CW00326827

Tips & Tricks
iPhone Secrets

intelligenti

intelligenti

St. Brandon's House

29 Great George Street, Bristol, BS1 5QT

http://www.intelligenti.com

© intelligenti 2013

Printed and bound in China

Introduction

Published by intelligenti, this book contains universal advice that can be used across all iPhone devices. Having sold over 2.5 million copies of its digital guides, intelligenti has now published the ultimate iPhone guide to establish itself as go-to source for iPhone advice and guidance.

This practical and accessible guide is an ideal tool to keep handy when you are trouble shooting or looking to get more from your device.

intelligenti continues to translate its guides into new languages and they are currently available in English, Spanish, Italian, German, French, Chinese, Japanese, and Portuguese.

intelligenti

Contents

CHAPTER 01
SHORTCUTS
GET THERE QUICKER

CHAPTER 02
ORGANIZE
KEEP NEAT AND TIDY

CHAPTER 03
BATTERY LIFE
KEEP IT ALIVE FOR LONGER

CHAPTER 04
TYPING
BECOME A KEYBOARD MASTER

CHAPTER 05
MUSIC
LISTEN TO YOUR MUSIC

CHAPTER 06
CAMERA
TAKE GREAT PICTURES

CHAPTER 07
PHOTOS
PICTURE THAT

CHAPTER 08
SAFARI
EXPLORE THE WEB

CHAPTER 09
MAIL
STAY IN TOUCH

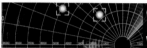

CHAPTER 10
SECURITY
KEEP YOUR DATA SAFE

CHAPTER 11
FIND MY PHONE
WHERE IS IT?

CHAPTER 12
iCLOUD
CONTROL YOUR BACKUP

CHAPTER 13
SIRI
YOUR PERSONAL ASSISTANT

CHAPTER 14
MICROPHONE
LOOK, NO HANDS

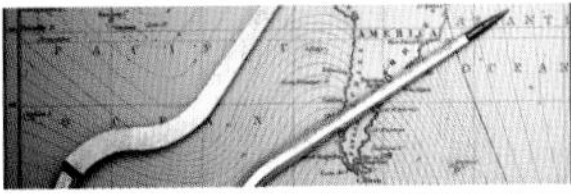

CHAPTER 15
MAPS
FIND YOUR WAY

CHAPTER 16
TRAVEL
AROUND THE WORLD

CHAPTER 17
ADVANCED
BECOME AN iPHONE GURU

CHAPTER 18
TROUBLESHOOTING
SOLVE THE PROBLEM

CHAPTER 19
HAVE YOU NOTICED
NEAT LITTLE TOUCHES

How to **Update Your iOS**

There are two ways to update your iPhone, either on your device or through iTunes.

To update on your iPhone, open *Settings*, *General*, and then *Software Update*. Tap **Download and Install** and wait for the update to download.

How to **Update Your iOS**

To update through iTunes, first ensure your computer is running the latest version.

To check you have the latest version, open iTunes on your computer. If you're using a Mac, go to the *iTunes* menu at the top and click *Check for Updates*. On Windows click *Help*, then *Check for Updates*.

How to **Update Your iOS**

Once you're running the latest version of iTunes, connect your iPhone using a USB cable. iTunes will then detect it and open a Summary page.

From this Summary page click **Check for Update**. This will check if an update is available and if there is one, you can install it on your iPhone.

iOS 4.2.1

A newer version of the iPhone softw
update your iPhone with the latest s

Update   Restor

250 million units of the iPhone have been sold in the first five years

CHAPTER ONE
SHORTCUTS

GET THERE QUICKER

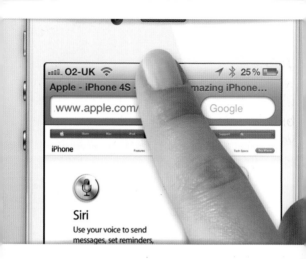

The Fast Way To The Top!

READING A WEB page, email, or SMS text message? In all of these applications, tap anywhere on the status bar at the top to quickly scroll to the head of that page.

This is especially handy in the *Messages* application if you want to call the person who has just sent you a text or picture.

Multitask

YOU CAN QUICKLY swap between apps without having to close the one you are using. Double press the Home button to bring up the multitasking bar. This reveals your apps in the order they were most recently opened. Swipe left to see more.

To access the app you want, simply tap on the icon.

Hidden Music Control

YOU CAN CONTROL music on your iPhone even while surfing the Internet or using other applications.

If a song is playing through *Music* (*iPod* prior to iOS 5) or any other app, double press the Home button to bring up the multitasking bar. Slide your finger to the right across the bar and music controls will appear.

Now you can skip or pause a song without exiting the app you're using.

Notification Center

THE NOTIFICATION CENTER allows you to see all your updates in one handy list.

To access the Notification Center, slide your finger down from the status bar.

You can also clear notifications. Tap the small cross and then Clear to keep only the most important app updates in Notification Center.

Notification Center Tab

IF YOU ARE in a full-screen app (when no status bar is showing), sliding your finger down from the top of the screen displays a small bar. This stops you accidentally opening Notification Center and interrupting the app you are using.

Tap and slide the small bar down to actually open Notification Center.

Quick Share

IF YOU'VE CONNECTED your Facebook or Twitter accounts to your iPhone, you can use Notification Center to update these accounts directly. Choose **Tap to Tweet** or **Tap to Post** to change your status. If you don't want these buttons showing, you can switch them off by going to *Settings*, *Notifications*, then *Share Widget*.

I'm Not **Speaking to You**

IT CAN BE embarrassing if your phone rings when you're in a meeting. Even if it's on silent, it might still be vibrating.

To immediately silence your phone, just tap one of the Volume buttons. To the caller, it seems like it's still ringing.

Send to **Voicemail**

YOU CAN SEND a call directly to voicemail by pressing the On/Off button on the top of the phone twice. You can also use the iPhone headset by quickly pressing the microphone button twice.

Now you can ignore people you don't want to talk to without letting your phone ring on and on.

Tap the
On/Off
button
twice

Respond to Calls

IF YOU RECEIVE a call when you are busy, but you want to respond with a text or call back later, slide the phone icon up and choose from the available options.

Select **Reply With Message** to send a default message to the caller, such as "What's up?" You can change them in *Settings*, *Phone*, *Reply With Message*.

Choose **Remind Me Later** to set up a reminder for a certain time or place so you remember to call back.

Redial

THERE IS A secret way to dial the last number typed into the keypad without having to enter the whole number again.

Open *Phone* and then select **Keypad**. Tap **Call** and the last number you dialed will appear at the top. Press **Call** again and the number will dial. While this is not quite an automatic redial, it's as close as you can get.

Rotation Lock

YOU CAN LOCK the screen in the portrait orientation so it doesn't accidentally rotate when placed on a table or when you're lying down.

Double tap the Home button to open the multitasking bar, and then slide to the right to reveal the rotation lock icon. Tap this and the screen will lock. To unlock it, just tap the icon again.

Back to the First Screen

IF YOU HAVE lots of pages of apps, scrolling backward and forward between them can take a while.

You don't have swipe through all the screens to get back to the start, though. To quickly return to the first screen of apps, just press the Home button.

Spotlight Search

SPOTLIGHT ENABLES YOU to search your phone for contacts, apps, music, video, audio books, notes, emails, calendar entries, and SMS messages.

Spotlight is located to the left of the first screen of apps. Just swipe to it, or press the Home button while you're on that first screen.

Quick Dial and Launch

IF YOU HAVE a lot of contacts or apps, locating and launching them can be much quicker using Spotlight.

In the Spotlight screen, just type in a few letters of the app or contact name. From the list, tap the person's name to call them or the icon to launch the app.

Rapid Web & Wiki Search

NEED SOME INFORMATION quickly? You can search the web and Wikipedia using Spotlight.

Type your search query into Spotlight and choose from **Search Wikipedia** or **Search Web**. Now you have a world of information at your fingertips.

Find Your Own Number

YOU CAN FIND your own phone number by opening the *Phone* app and going to the **Contacts** tab.

Swipe down on the list of contacts to reveal your phone number above the search box at the top.

Take a **Screenshot**

IF YOU WANT to save images from apps, you can take a screenshot of the current screen on your iPhone. To do this, press the Home and On/Off buttons at the same time. The screen will flash and the camera sound will play.

You can view the screenshot in the Camera Roll album in the *Photos* app.

Press the Home and On/Off buttons together

Slide Notifications

SOMETIMES APP UPDATES appear as notifications on your Lock screen. You can open the app and go directly to the update from these notifications.

To do so, slide the app icon to the right, just like you slide to unlock the screen.

Nine rare minerals are used to make the iPhone vibrate, play music, show color on its screen, and do all the cool things we love it for

CHAPTER TWO
ORGANIZE

KEEP NEAT AND TIDY

Move or Delete Apps

IT IS EASY to move the icons around on your iPhone and delete those apps that you no longer use.

Hold your finger on one of the apps for a couple of seconds and they will all start to shake.

You can now drag them around to rearrange. The little ⊗ icon on the corner of downloaded apps allows you to delete them and free up space for new ones.

Delete Single Calls

YOU CAN DELETE individual phone calls from your call history. Open the *Phone* app and tap Recents. Swipe across a call entry with your finger to reveal a **Delete** button, tap this and the call will disappear.

To delete all entries, tap the **Edit** button and then the **Clear** button. Tap **Clear All Recents** and the list will be emptied.

Folders

IT CAN SOMETIMES be useful to group together similar apps. To keep things really organized, you can create folders that will hold up to 12 apps.

While moving apps, drag one app on top of another to create a folder. You can name this so you know what apps are in it. The folder can be moved around in the same way as the apps. You can even place a folder in the dock at the bottom of the screen.

Check App Size and Delete

IF YOUR PHONE is low on storage, you might want to know what's taking up all the space. To find out, open *Settings*, *General*, then *Usage*.

This shows all your apps, music, and videos. Tap an app to see how much space it's using, then **Delete App** to free up space.

It took over 200 patents and 156 suppliers across three continents to make the first iPhone

CHAPTER THREE
BATTERY LIFE

KEEP IT ALIVE
FOR LONGER

Turn Off Connections

YOU CAN SAVE battery power to make your iPhone last while using other features by turning off the individual connections that your phone automatically makes.

Open *Settings*, *Wi-Fi*, and turn it off to stop the Wi-Fi connection.

To turn off 3G, open *Settings*, *General*, *Mobile Data* (before iOS 6, *General*, *Network*) and turn off *Enable 3G*. Note that this will make your internet connection slower.

To turn off Bluetooth, open *Settings*, *Bluetooth* (before iOS 6, *General*, *Bluetooth*) and turn it off.

To disable all connections at once, turn on **Airplane Mode** from *Settings*.

Turn Off Push Email

KEEPING PUSH EMAIL turned off can save quite a lot of juice, particularly in areas with a poor signal.

Go to *Settings*, *Mail…*, *Fetch New Data*. Turn off **Push** and set Fetch to **Manually**.

To receive email with both Push and Fetch switched off, just open the *Mail* app.

Keep It Cool

THE PHONE LASTS longer when kept between 0° and 35°C (32° to 95°F). Outside this range battery life can suffer, so try not to leave your phone in a glovebox or on a parcel shelf in summer.

Using a case that doesn't give your phone air can also lead to decreased battery life. If it gets really hot, you'll see a warning message.

Turn Off Location

SOME APPS, SUCH as *Maps* or *Camera*, request the use of your current location, which can run the battery down. If an app is using your location, an arrow will be displayed in the status bar.

To see which apps are using your location, open **Settings**, *Privacy*, *Location Services* (before iOS 6, open **Settings**, *Location Services*). You can turn off all location services at the top, or individually.

Turn off Local Weather

WITH IOS 5 and later you can have the local forecast showing in Notification Center. However, every time you open it, the iPhone looks for your location, which uses more battery power.

To stop this, open the *Weather* app, tap the 'i', and turn off **Local Weather**. Notification Center will then only update the forecast and no longer look for your location.

Battery Life Percentage

IF YOU HAVE an iPhone 3GS or later you can add a percentage battery-life indicator to the status bar.

This is enabled via *Settings*, *General*, then *Usage*, and gives a more accurate idea of the battery power you have left.

No Lock Screen Notifications

NOTIFICATIONS CAN APPEAR on the Lock screen, but they turn on the screen and use some battery power.

To turn them off, open *Settings* then *Notifications*. Here is a list of the apps which can update you. Tap an app, scroll down and turn off **View in Lock Screen**.

You can tap **Notifications** in the top left to return to the list of apps in order to change the others. Note that you can't turn them all off together—they have to be done individually.

Battery Draining Apps

IF YOU FIND that your battery is running down quickly, it may be because certain types of apps are running even when they are not open.

Internet phone-call apps such as Skype, apps using your location, music-playing apps, apps using Newsstand, and those connected with an external accessory use up more battery power, so close these first to see if it improves.

To check for open apps, access the multitasking bar. Close the apps by tapping and holding the icons, then tap the minus sign.

Dim the Screen

THE SCREEN IS one of the most significant drains on the battery. You can reduce the amount of power the screen uses by turning down the brightness. Open *Settings*, then *Brightness*, and move the slider to make the screen darker.

You can also set the auto-lock time to turn off the screen automatically. Open *Settings*, *General*, then *Auto-Lock*. Select a shorter time to use less power.

Apple spent $150 million developing the first iPhone prototype

CHAPTER FOUR
TYPING

BECOME A
KEYBOARD MASTER

Hold Shift While Typing

SOMETIMES WHEN TYPING, you just need the next few letters to be capitalized, for example, "My PC is BROKEN!" or for abbreviations such as "LOL." The phone allows you to use the Shift key just as on a computer; simply hold it down with one finger while you type with another.

Slide for Capitals

ENTERING ALL CAPITALS by tapping shift and then tapping the letter can take a long time. To quickly enter a capital just tap and hold the Shift button. Now drag your finger over to the letter you want and let go.

This capitalizes only that letter and you can carry on typing as normal. This is useful for typing place names like New York or London.

Slide to Punctuate

TO QUICKLY ENTER punctuation or numbers from the keyboard, tap and hold the button with **123** on it. Keeping your finger on the screen, slide to any number or punctuation button.

When you release your finger, that character will be inserted and the usual keyboard reappears.

Emoji Emoticons

YOU CAN ADD Emoji emoticons as a keyboard. Open **Settings**, *General*, *Keyboards*, then *International Keyboards*. Find the Emoji option and tap to add it as a keyboard.

Then when you type, tap the small globe next to the space bar to get the icons. 😀

Shake to Undo and Redo

WHEN TYPING IN any application, or when using cut, copy, and paste, you can shake the phone to undo your typing and shake again to redo. Your phone will pop up a query to double check.

Double-Tap for Shift Lock

THE TITLE HERE says it all, but this feature is disabled by default. To enable, open *Settings*, *General*, then *Keyboard*, and turn on **Enable Caps Lock**.

Now you can double tap the Shift key to turn on caps lock. The key will turn blue when locked.

Hold Keys for Extras!

IF YOU HOLD down certain letters or punctuation on the keyboard, a pop-up appears containing other options. For example, you can hold down the currency symbol to get other currencies.

Cut, Copy, and Paste

YOU CAN CUT, copy, and paste text from web pages, notes, and SMS messages between applications.

Double tap or hold down on text and then wait for the **Copy** button to appear. To paste this text, tap once where you would like it to appear and then tap the **Paste** option. This is a great way to copy a website address from *Safari* and then paste it into *Mail*.

Get a **Bigger Keyboard**

TURNING YOUR PHONE sideways will enlarge the keyboard in all standard applications, including *Notes*, *Messages*, *Mail*, and *Safari*. In *Safari*, as soon as you begin editing the address the orientation will lock, so turn your phone sideways before tapping the address bar.

Hide Message Keyboard

WHEN READING MESSAGES it can be hard to view the conversation when the keyboard blocks half the screen.

Slide your finger down from above the text-entry box and the keyboard starts to disappear. Carry on until only the text-entry box is left. To make the keyboard reappear, tap the text-entry box.

Get a **Magnifying Glass**

MOST APPS PROVIDE a magnifying glass for editing and selecting text. To access this, just place your finger over the text for a second.

This is useful for positioning the cursor in the right place or when selecting a particular word for copying, providing more precise control.

Quickly Insert a Period

IF YOU TAP the space bar twice, the iPhone inserts a period (full stop) followed by a single space. You can also do this by tapping the space bar with two fingers at the same time.

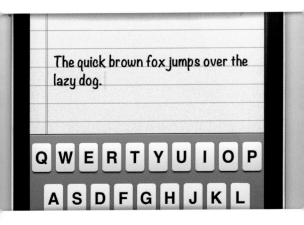

What if you actually want two spaces? Simply tap once then wait for a couple of seconds before tapping again.

Quick Correct

WHEN TYPING, YOU may find that you enter a word incorrectly or that auto-correct changes it when you tap the space bar.

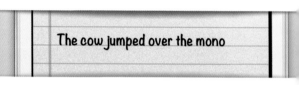

Instead of deleting the whole word, just tap the backspace key once to see the replacement options, then select the word you want to change it to.

Typing Shortcuts

YOU CAN CREATE custom typing shortcuts to quickly add common phrases to messages, such as "On my way!"

Open *Settings*, *General*, then *Keyboard*. Here you will find the **Shortcuts** section. Tap **Add New Shortcut...** and then enter the phrase and shortcut you want.

When typing in apps, you can input the shortcut and the iPhone will offer to auto-complete the full phrase for you. Tap the space bar to complete the phrase and carry on typing.

SMS Character Count

YOU CAN TURN on an SMS character count to see the length of your message. This is useful, as messages that are more than 160 characters long are billed as multiple texts.

Open *Settings* then *Messages* and turn on **Character Count**. The count appears after you have typed one line. This doesn't appear when sending an iMessage as your character count is unlimited.

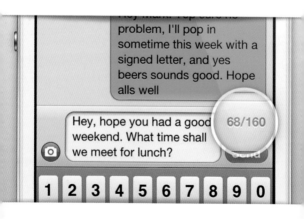

Add Words to Dictionary

IF YOU FIND yourself being corrected a lot while typing, you might want to add some new words to the dictionary so that your iPhone recognizes them.

To do so, open **Settings**, *General*, then *Keyboard*. Scroll down to **Shortcuts** and tap **Add New Shortcut**.

Type the word into the Phrase box and leave the Shortcut box empty. Tap **Save** in the top right. Now your iPhone won't try to correct you when typing that word.

Dictation

IF YOU HAVE the iPhone 4S, you can use dictation to type out messages for you. To do this, tap the microphone key next to the space bar and start speaking. Once you are finished, just tap **Done**.

To include punctuation, just speak it. For example, for the sentence "Hey, how are you today?" you would say, "Hey comma how are you today question mark."

You can even add paragraphs by saying "new paragraph."

*Apple released
the first iPhone
on June 29, 2007*

CHAPTER FIVE
MUSIC

LISTEN TO YOUR MUSIC

AirPlay

YOU CAN STREAM your music and videos through Apple TV using AirPlay.

From the *Music* or *Videos* (*iPod* prior to iOS 5) apps press the AirPlay icon. Both devices must be connected to the same Wi-Fi network for this to work.

AirPlay Mirroring

IF YOU HAVE an iPhone 4S and an Apple TV box you can stream your display to share photos, use apps, etc. on a bigger screen.

The best way to do this is from the multitasking bar. Press the Home button twice and swipe the bar to the right for volume controls. Tap the AirPlay icon and turn on Mirroring. Return here to turn it off again.

Multitask Volume

YOU CAN QUICKLY change the volume of your iPhone through the multitasking bar.

Double press the Home button to open the multitasking bar. Swipe right once to see the playback controls and then swipe right again to reveal the volume controls.

Delete Songs

WANT TO OVERHAUL your music to free up some space? You can delete songs, artists, or albums from within the *Music* app.

When viewing a list of songs, artists, or albums, swipe across the name to reveal the **Delete** button. Tap this to remove the song from your iPhone.

Cover Flow

WHILE USING THE *Music* app and viewing the Now Playing information, turn your iPhone sideways to activate Cover Flow. This shows the cover artwork for all your music. Swipe left or right to view your library.

Touching the artwork opens the song list. From here you can select a track and start playing it.

Stop Speaker Interference

WHEN YOU DOCK your phone into speakers that don't specifically support the iPhone, it detects this and advises that you may experience interference.

To stop any possible interference turn on Airplane Mode from *Settings*. This stops the cellular data interrupting playback.

Shake to Shuffle

WHILE PLAYING MUSIC, shaking your phone shuffles to another track at random. The phone disables this when listening to podcasts or audio books. Shuffling works while the *Music* app is running, when the controls are displayed in the multitasking bar *(see Tip 3,)* or on the lock screen.

You can disable shuffle altogether through *Settings*, then *Music*.

32% of iPhone users have downloaded a game for their phone

CHAPTER SIX
CAMERA

TAKE GREAT PICTURES

Press Volume Up

WHEN USING THE *Camera* app, tapping the shutter icon on the screen to take a photo can cause you to shake and lose focus.

Instead, press the Volume Up button on the side of your iPhone to take a picture. This lets you hold the phone like a normal camera, which gives you more stability to take a great picture.

Slide for Camera Roll

WHILE USING THE *Camera* app you can quickly access the Camera Roll by sliding your finger from left to right across the screen. Keep sliding to scroll through all your recent photos.

You don't have to scroll back through all your shots to start taking photos again. Just tap the screen, then tap the blue camera icon.

Open From Lock Screen

IF YOUR PHONE is locked, there is a shortcut to quickly open the *Camera* app: tap and hold the camera icon then swipe upwards.

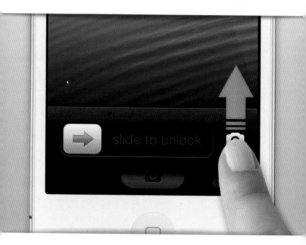

An added security feature while using the camera like this is that you can only view the photos you take. This is to stop anyone from looking through your entire photo history.

Camera Focus

WHILE TAKING A picture, you can tap the screen on the part of the image you want to focus on. This can be a close-up item or one farther away.

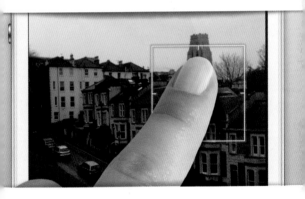

The iPhone will automatically focus to that point for a clearer picture or video.

With iOS 4 and later, you also have a digital zoom. Pinch the screen or drag the slider to zoom in.

Panorama

TAKE GREAT PICTURES of wide vistas with the new Panorama mode on the iPhone 4S and 5.

Open the *Camera* app, tap **Options**, then **Panorama**. A rectangular box then appears across the middle of the screen with an arrow. You can swap the direction of the panorama by tapping the arrow. Once you start the shot, the arrow helps you keep level as you pan. Tap the camera icon to stop the shot.

Move iPhone continuously when taking a Panorama.

"We're gambling on our vision, and we would rather do that than make 'me too' products. Let some other companies do that. For us, it's always the next dream"

Steve Jobs

CHAPTER SEVEN
PHOTOS

PICTURE THAT

Create Photo Albums

YOU CAN CREATE photo albums from the *Photos* app. On the Albums page tap the + button (before iOS 6, **Edit**, then **Add**).

Name the album and add photos from the Camera Roll by tapping them. Once the photos are selected, tap **Done** to create the album. If you want to delete the album, tap **Edit** and a minus icon will appear next to the album, allowing you to remove it.

Add to Albums

IF YOU WANT to add more photos to your albums later, just access the Camera Roll.

In the thumbnail view, tap the **Edit** button (before iOS 6, the  icon) and select the pictures you want to add to an album.

Tap the **Add To** button at the bottom and choose **Add to Existing Album** or **Add to New Album**.

GeoTagging

WHEN YOU TAKE a photo, your iPhone tags the picture with the location where it was taken.

You can view your photos by location in the *Photos* app. Tap the **Places** tab to reveal a map with all your photos on. Now you can find your holiday snaps without having to search through all your photos.

Photo Stream

YOU CAN USE Photo Stream to share your most recently taken photos with all your other Apple devices.

Open *Settings*, *iCloud*, and check that *Photo Stream* is turned on. To view the photos being shared, open *Photos* and select the tab Photo Stream.

With iOS 5.1 and later, you can delete photos from Photo Stream and it will remove them from all devices.

Shared Photo Stream

SHARE PICTURES WITH friends or family by creating a Shared Photo Stream.

To create one, open *Photos* and open your *Camera Roll* album. Tap the **Edit** button and select the images you want to share. Then tap the Share button and choose Photo Stream. Add your recipients, name the album, and decide if it will be publicly available on iCloud. Tap **Create** and the pictures will be shared.

Send Multiple Photos

YOU CAN SEND pictures via MMS, or via email from the *Photos* app.

To select them, tap the **Edit** button (before iOS 6, the  icon), tap the photos and then **Share**.

Tap the **Mail** option to send via email. You can share up to five photos via email, but beyond that you can only copy the images.

"[Design is] not just
what it looks like and
feels like. Design is how
it works"
Steve Jobs

CHAPTER EIGHT
SAFARI

EXPLORE THE WEB

Plain Lazy Web Surfing

IF YOU'RE HEADING for a .com domain when typing an address in *Safari*, you don't have to type the www or the .com. For example, you can enter "apple" in the address box to view www.apple.com.

The Secret Behind .com

WHEN TYPING AN address in *Safari*, the .com key hides some additional options.

If you hold your finger on it for a second, a range of alternatives appear. Slide your finger to one and release. The .com key is only available when typing website addresses in *Safari*.

Look Before You Leap!

TO SEE WHERE a web page link will direct you, simply hold your finger on it for a second.

A menu appears that lists the actual address at the top and some additional options. You can copy the address and paste the link in a new page.

Just the Right Size

WHEN BROWSING WEB pages in *Safari*, you can double tap on a column, word, or picture to fit its width to your screen. Double tap again to zoom out.

Save Safari Images

IMAGES SHOWN IN *Safari* can be saved to your phone's Camera Roll or copied to the clipboard. You can then set them as your wallpaper, send via email, or apply to a contact.

Hold your finger on an image until the options slide up. Tap **Copy** to place the image on the clipboard or **Save Image** to save to your Camera Roll.

Create New App Icons

YOU CAN ADD a new app icon for any website to your home screen.

While browsing in *Safari*, tap the  icon and then tap **Add to Home Screen**. Some websites supply an icon, for others, a shot of the current view is used. Tapping the icon launches *Safari* and immediately takes you to the website.

Share Links with Friends

STUMBLED ACROSS A web page you really want to share? Simply tap the  icon at the bottom of the screen and select from the available options.

Reading List

YOU CAN USE *Safari* to create a list of articles that you want to read later. To add an article, tap the  icon and tap **Add to Reading List**.

To view it, tap the icon and then **Reading List**. Tap an article to go to that website again.

If you enable iCloud syncing, the articles will also be added to *Safari* on your other devices.

Search on Page

YOU CAN SEARCH for certain words on the page while using *Safari*.

To do so, start typing the word in the search box. At the bottom an option **On This Page will appear**. Tap **Find "word"** to find the first instance of that word.

You can then press **Next** to advance to the next instance of the word. This way you can quickly go to the part of the page you're looking for.

Private Browsing

BROWSE THE INTERNET without the sites you visit being recorded in your history. This is perfect to search for gifts online without the risk of significant others finding out.

To enable, open **Settings**, *Safari*, and turn on *Private Browsing*. Open **Safari** and you will see that the toolbars are now dark. To return to normal, open **Settings**, *Safari*, *Private Browsing* again and turn it off.

Fullscreen View

WHILE USING *SAFARI* in landscape view, the viewing space can seem restricted by the toolbars.

To increase the view to full screen, tap the icon on the right of the toolbar.

Quick History

MAKE YOUR WAY around the internet quickly by using a shortcut to open up your history.

Tap and hold the back button to see your history. This shows you all the websites you have recently visited. Tap on any of the websites to jump to that page again.

---

*In the first five years,
Apple sold 250 million
units of the iPhone*

CHAPTER NINE
MAIL

STAY IN TOUCH

Swipe to Delete

WHILE VIEWING MOST lists there is a hidden way to delete items.

Simply swipe across the email, note, or SMS conversation and a handy **Delete** button appears.

This also works in many other apps, including *Music* and *Notes*.

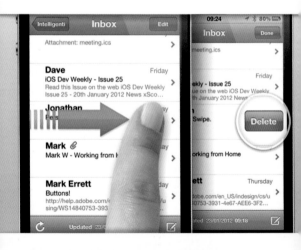

Delete Multiple Emails

TO DELETE MORE than one email at a time, tap the **Edit** button, then tap on the clear circles next to each email to select them.

Finally, tap **Delete** at the bottom of the screen to remove them from your inbox.

The Secret Behind the Dot

WHEN TYPING AN email address in the *Mail* app or *Safari*, the . key hides additional options.

IF YOU HOLD your finger on the dot for a second, a range of useful shortcuts appear. Simply slide your finger to the one you want and then release.

Email Signature

WANT TO ADD some personality or useful contact details to your "Sent from my iPhone" email signature?

Go to **Settings**, *Mail…*, *Signature*. Here you can delete your current signature and type a new one, perhaps including a website link, your Twitter name, or your company name.

If you have iOS 6 installed, you can change the signature for each address. Tap **Per Account** and edit them individually.

Flag **Mail**

YOU CAN EASILY keep track of your important emails by flagging them. To flag an email, tap the  icon on the toolbar.

You can also mark multiple emails from the Inbox. Tap **Edit** and then tap on the circle next to each email. Tap **Mark** at the bottom and select **Flag**. You'll now see a small flag icon next to these emails in your Inbox.

Back to Your Draft Message

YOU CAN QUICKLY return to your most recent draft email when looking through the *Mail* app.

Tap and hold the new email icon for a few seconds and the last draft you were working on will appear. With iOS 6 and later, you can choose which of your draft messages to open.

Highlight and Reply

IF YOU RECEIVE a long email and wish to reply or forward a specific section, there is no need to include the entire message.

If you highlight part of the message before replying or forwarding, only that selection will appear in the new email.

Format Options

DRAW ATTENTION TO certain sections of your email by formatting them. Double tap a word to select it, and then tap the right arrow.

Here you'll find the option **B**/<u>U</u>. Tap this and select **Bold**, **Italics**, or **Underline**. If you want, you can select all three.

VIP Inbox

MAKING CERTAIN CONTACTS VIPs means you can collect all your email exchanges with those contacts in a separate VIP inbox.

Open *Mail*, tap *VIP*, and then choose the contacts you want to add.

Once you've selected your VIPs, you can enable custom alerts for these emails by tapping *VIP Alerts*. Assign a different sound from your normal email alert so you know when a VIP email has arrived!

Different Account Sounds

IF YOU USE several email accounts, you can assign each account a separate alert sound, so you know which one has received an email.

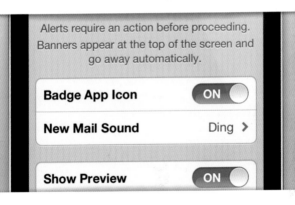

To control the different sounds, open *Settings*, *Notifications*, and tap *Mail*. Select an account and change the *New Mail Sound* for each one. Now you can ignore those work emails over the weekend.

Pull to Refresh Inbox

TO SEE IF you have any new mail, refresh your Inbox. To do so, pull down from the top of the screen until the refresh icon starts to spin.

The *Mail* app will then check for any new emails and download them to your Inbox.

Insert **Photo & Video**

INSERT A PICTURE you have taken or video you have recorded directly into an email from within the *Mail* app.

Tap the screen where you are entering text and wait for the options to appear. Press the right arrow twice, then tap **Insert Photo & Video**. Choose which picture or video you want to add from your Camera Roll.

Rearrange **Mailboxes**

IT IS POSSIBLE to change the order of your Inboxes in the *Mail* app. This means that you can place the most important Inbox at the top for easier access.

Tap **Edit** and then move an Inbox around by dragging on the three small lines next to it. Tap **Done** to save the order.

Delete Instead of Archive

IF YOU ARE using a Gmail account in *Mail*, it archives rather than deletes an email. To delete a message, tap and hold the 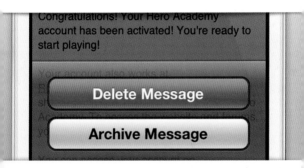 icon until you see **Delete Message**.

Congratulations! Your Hero Academy account has been activated! You're ready to start playing!

Delete Message

Archive Message

If you would always prefer to delete messages, you can disable archiving from **Settings** then *Mail, Contacts, Calendars*. Tap on your Gmail account name and turn off *Archive Messages*.

Remove **from Recents**

WHEN ENTERING A recipient's email address, recently used addresses show automatically to save you time. However, sometimes these can be incorrect and annoying.

To remove a recently used email address, tap the blue arrow icon next to the entry and then **Remove from Recents**.

"*I'm actually as proud of the things we haven't done as the things I have done. Innovation is saying 'no' to 1,000 things*"
Steve Jobs

CHAPTER TEN
SECURITY

80 90 100
70
60
50
40
30 20

KEEP YOUR DATA SAFE

Parental Controls

RESTRICTIONS ALLOW YOU to stop certain actions being performed on the iPhone, so you can feel safe when handing it over to your kids.

Open *Settings*, *General*, *Restrictions*. Tap **Enable Restrictions** and then enter a passcode. Remember this, as you will need it to turn the options back on.

From Restrictions, you can turn off apps such as *YouTube*, *iTunes*, and *App Store*, among others.

You can also stop apps from being accidentally deleted by turning off the **Deleting Apps** option. It's also possible to prevent In-App purchases by turning off the relevant option.

Keep Your Data Secure

ENABLE A PASSCODE to avoid unwanted access by family, friends—or a thief.

Open *Settings*, *General*, *Passcode Lock*. Tap **Turn Passcode On** and enter a memorable four-digit passcode.

With iOS 4 and later, you can create a more secure passcode. Turning off **Simple Passcode** allows you to select a longer passcode that includes letters as well as numbers.

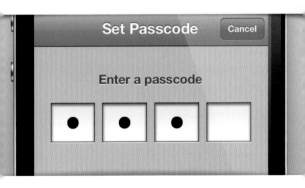

Erase All Data

THE IPHONE OFFERS additional security to keep your data safe from prying eyes if your device is stolen.

From *Settings*, *General*, *Passcode Lock*, turn on **Erase All Data**. If someone tries to guess your passcode, the iPhone erases all data after 10 unsuccessful attempts.

Check Your Privacy

SOME APPS CAN access your location, contacts, calendar events, reminders, and pictures. To check which apps are using these, open *Settings* then *Privacy*.

Look into each option to see which apps are accessing those details. You can turn this function off in each app if you don't want them to have this access. Note that this might affect their usability, though.

"*Being the richest man in the cemetery doesn't matter to me... Going to bed at night saying we've done something wonderful... that's what matters to me*"
Steve Jobs

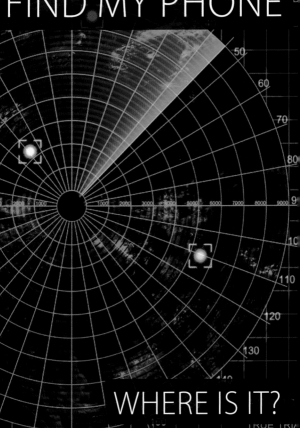

CHAPTER ELEVEN
FIND MY PHONE

WHERE IS IT?

Find My iPhone...

WHEN YOU UPDATE to iOS 5 you can turn on the **Find My iPhone** option when you set up your device. If you did not activate this at set-up, open *Settings*, *iCloud*, and turn on **Find My iPhone**.

You can then go to www.icloud.com on a computer and select **Find My iPhone** to reveal its location. You'll be given several options to help find your phone, which are explained on the next few pages.

Play a Sound

ONCE YOUR DEVICE is located, select it to see the available options. Choose **Play Sound** to have your iPhone emit an audible alert.

If the device is nearby you'll be able to hear it and can determine its location. Once you find it you can dismiss the on-screen alert.

Lost Mode

YOU CAN ENABLE Lost Mode from www.icloud.com. This allows you to lock the phone, show a phone number on the screen and then let whoever finds your device call that number.

From the website you can also see how much battery charge is remaining. The online map also updates the route it is taking and you can track it down—with the help of the police of course!

Remotely Wipe Your Data

IF YOUR PHONE contains sensitive data, you can wipe it and reset it to its factory settings. Select **Erase iPhone** from the possible options.

Your iPhone will no longer be able to respond to location requests, so you'll need to decide between keeping your data secure or having access to information on the phone's location.

If you are reunited with your phone, you can use *iTunes* or iCloud to restore the data from your last secure backup.

Find Your iPhone App

YOU CAN USE the *Find My iPhone* app on the iPhone to locate other devices, including your iPad, iPod touch, and Mac.

On iPad and iPod touch you need to be on iOS 5 and make sure the **Find My...** option is enabled from *Settings*, *iCloud*. If you have a Mac with OS X 10.7.2 or later, turn on the **Find My...** from *System Preferences*, *iCloud*.

"Everybody in our company is responsible to be innovative, whether they're doing operational work or product work or customer service work"
Tim Cook,
Apple CEO

CHAPTER TWELVE
iCLOUD

CONTROL YOUR BACKUP

What is iCloud?

ICLOUD ALLOWS YOU to share items between your devices.

From *Settings* then *iCloud* you can select which basic items you want shared across your devices.

For example, if you create an event in the *Reminders* app on your iPhone, it will also appear in the *Reminders* app on your iPad without needing to sync.

How Much Space?

IF YOU RECEIVE a warning that you are using too much space in iCloud, you can control which apps are backed up.

Open *Settings*, *iCloud*, *Storage & Backup*. This shows you how much space is available. Tap **Manage Storage** and then the device you are using to check.

This shows which apps take up the most room in your iCloud and you can decide which items you do want to backup.

Automatic Downloads

IF YOU HAVE automatic downloads turned on, any time you download songs, apps, or books, they will also appear on your other devices without having to sync.

To turn this on, open *Settings*, then *Store*. Turn on the items you would like to be downloaded automatically.

It took 74 days to reach 1 million sales of the original iPhone

CHAPTER THIRTEEN
SIRI

YOUR PERSONAL ASSISTANT

Introduction to Siri

SIRI IS A personal assistant that resides on the iPhone 4S and iPhone 5. Siri responds to the words you speak rather than what you type. While you can talk to your iPhone 4S or 5 to perform a range of tasks, you'll also hear Siri's human-like voice talk back at you to confirm it's understood.

Siri was first introduced in September, 2011 with iOS 5.0 and is only available if you have an iPhone 4S or iPhone 5.

Enable Siri

IF YOU DID not turn on Siri while setting up your iPhone 4S or 5, you can activate it by opening *Settings*, *General*, *Siri*.

Siri is your personal assistant, and can be used to control certain functions on your phone by voice command. To access Siri, press and hold the Home button for a few seconds until the microphone icon appears, and then start speaking after you hear the double beep.

Commands for Siri

YOU CAN USE Siri to send messages to friends, create a reminder, call contacts, set an alarm, and much more.

If you need a reminder of all the things Siri can do, just tap 🛈 when you are using it.

Siri Settings

YOU CAN ALSO activate Siri by lifting the phone to your ear. This helps it hear you more clearly, but leaving this function on can drain the battery.

To turn it off, open *Settings*, *General*, *Siri*. Turn off **Raise to Speak** and you will only be able to use Siri by pressing and holding the Home button.

Advanced Contact Details

ADDING EXTRA CONTACT details can help Siri know more about you.

Start Siri and then say the contact name followed by their relationship to you—for example, "John Appleseed is my brother." Siri will then ask you to confirm the relationship.

You can add all types of relationships, including, mother, partner, siblings, and more. We've even added our nemesis so we can dial them up quickly!

Tell Siri About Yourself

ONCE SIRI KNOWS who you are, it can set up reminders at addresses associated with your entry in the **contacts** listing.

Open **Settings**, *General*, *Siri*. Tap **My Info** and select your contact entry.

You can say "Remind me to take out the trash when I get home," and Siri will set the reminder to go off at that location.

If you have set your father, mother, or partner, you can say "call Mom" or "email boyfriend" and it will know whom to contact straight away.

Some Quirky Siri Commands

THEY MAY NOT do much, but it's always fun to see the results of these commands:

- "How much wood could a woodchuck chuck?"

- "Open the pod bay doors"

- "I love you!"

- "What is the meaning of life?"

- "Tell me a story"

- "What are you wearing?"

- "Knock knock"

- "Will you marry me?"

- "What's your favorite color?"

Find Me **That...**

SIRI HAS SOME more options with iOS 6. You can now find out the sport results, and look up movie listings. Try out these commands:

- "What was the Nationals score?"

- "Did Manchester United win yesterday?"

- "What's showing at my local theater?"

- "Which films star Christian Bale?"

The Nationals beat the Giants by a score of 9 to 4 last Wednesday.

NATIONALS PARK

4 - 9

1 2 3 4 5 6 7 8 9 R H E

Open Your Apps

YOU CAN OPEN your favorite apps with Siri. For example, say, "Open Instagram" and the app will open straight away.

If you have apps with similar names, Siri will present all the possible options and you can choose which app to open.

A Siri List

YOU CAN USE *Reminders* to create a grocery list. To start a new list, open *Reminders*, tap the ▤ icon in the top left, then **Edit**. Tap **Create New List…** and enter its name, for example 'Groceries,' and then tap **Done**.

While using Siri, you can say, "Add milk to Groceries list" to add an item to that list. We've started lists for gifts, favorite bands, places to eat, and movies to watch.

The iPhone 4 clocked 600,000 pre-orders in just a single day

CHAPTER FOURTEEN
MICROPHONE

LOOK, NO HANDS

Control Calls

THE EARBUDS THAT come with the iPhone have a built-in microphone you can use for hands-free calling. The microphone is also a button—squeeze it and you'll hear a click.

When your phone is ringing, click the button once to answer the call. To reject the call, press and hold the button for two seconds, then release it. At the end of a phone conversation, click once to end the call.

...**Control Calls** Continued

IF YOU ARE already on a call and another one comes in, you can click the microphone button once to switch to the new call. Click again to go back to the original call.

To end the current call and switch to the new one, press and hold the button for two seconds then let go.

With the iPhone 3GS, 4, 4S, and 5, you can use the Volume buttons to change the volume of the call.

Controlling Music Playback

YOU CAN ALSO use the mic button to control playback of music or videos.

Click once to pause the current song or video and then click again to resume.

Quickly click twice to skip to the next song or quickly click three times to go back to the previous song. If you are more than three seconds into the current track, clicking three times will restart it.

Take a Picture

IF YOU HAVE updated to iOS 5, you can use the Volume Up button on the inline mic to take a picture while using the *Camera* app. This allows you to hold the iPhone steady, or place it on a tripod and use the earbud button to control taking the picture.

If you have a Bluetooth headset, you can also press the Volume Up button on this to take the photo remotely. Now you can get the perfect group shot.

Voice Control

IF YOU HAVE an iPhone 3GS or iPhone 4, you can use Voice Control to make calls and play music.

To access Voice Control, press and hold the Home button or middle button on the earbuds for about three seconds, then speak your command.

You can even ask "What time is it?" and your phone will tell you.

154   Tips & Tricks

Improve Voice Control

MOST PHONES CONTAIN some contacts that are stored by their first name only.

You'll find that the command *"Call Joanna Smith"* works a lot better than just *"Call Jo,"* so expand abbreviations and add last names to your contacts wherever possible.

You can also add a nickname via the 'add field' option in **Contacts**. You can then say "Call Papa", for example, to start calling your father.

There have been over 30 billion apps downloaded as of June, 2012

CHAPTER FIFTEEN
MAPS

FIND YOUR WAY

Hidden **Compass**

WHILE USING THE *Maps* app you can quickly find your current location. Tap the  icon in the bottom left and the map zooms to where you are.

Pressing this again turns on the compass, so you can tell which direction you're facing. This is great if you're lost in an unfamiliar place.

3D View

TO GET A different view of an area, tap the
3D button.

The angle then
shifts to give you
an overview of
that location.
This can be
especially handy
when looking
at possible
directions and
aids in getting
your bearings,
along with
the hidden
compass feature
as described
opposite.

Traffic Report

THE MAPS APP lets you see any traffic problems on the route you plan to take. Tap the page curl in the bottom right and choose the Show Traffic option.

This reveals traffic data on the map. Roads highlighted with a red dashed line indicate bad traffic. The map also shows the location of roadworks, road closures, and accidents.

Hidden Gestures

THERE ARE SOME simple finger gestures you can use to make the most of *Maps*.

Tap the screen with two fingers to zoom out by one level. Place two fingers on screen together and move them up or down to change the angle of your view.

To rotate the view, place two fingers apart on screen and twist them. To return to the default view, tap the compass icon in the top right.

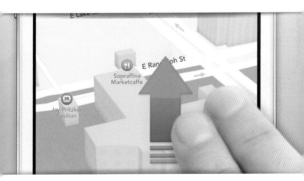

Share Your Location

TO HELP YOU organize a meeting place, why not use *Maps* to share a location with friends or family?

Tap on any pin, including your current location, and then the blue arrow.

Tap **Share Location** and choose from the options. This sends a link to your location that the recipient can open in *Maps*.

Not **Driving?**

YOU CAN FIND recommended apps to use for public transit help from *Maps*. While looking for directions, tap the bus icon to see a list of apps relevant to your current location that can help you.

You can also tap the stick-figure icon to get rough walking directions to your destination. However, be aware that these might send you down major roads without the safety of a sidewalk.

Quick **Route**

YOU CAN ALSO get quick directions to any point on the map.

Tap on a location icon or pin, and wait for the info box to appear. From here tap the Quick Route icon. Choose from the possible routes and tap Start.

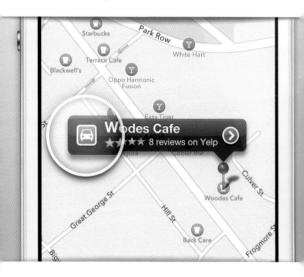

See **Reviews**

YOU CAN SEE reviews from Yelp! for many businesses. Tap on a location icon to get info about it, then tap the blue arrow. Select **Reviews** to see what others have said about that place, or tap **Photos** to see pictures.

More information about the location is given at the top of the screen. This includes opening hours, how far it is from your location, and if it's a restaurant, the average cost of a meal.

Info	Reviews	Photos

★★★★☆ by Gabrielle R. 23/04/2012

I am very happy with this restaurant. It's very casual (definitely kid-friendly), has a great selection of food, and I've always fo… >

★★★★☆ by Kat T. 22/04/2012

-great beer
-great pizzas
-great sandwich selection… >

★★★★☆ by Kelly P. 16/04/2012

Over 80% of iPhone users use their phone over 15 times a day

CHAPTER SIXTEEN
TRAVEL

AROUND THE WORLD

Reduce **Roaming Charges**

3G USE OVERSEAS can be an expensive luxury, but there are a few ways to reduce the costs.

Data roaming can run up huge bills, so turn it off from *Settings*, *General*, *Cellular (Network in some countries.)*

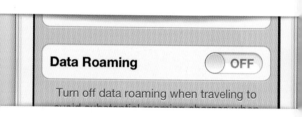

Data Roaming OFF

Turn off data roaming when traveling to

If you need to use your cell connection while abroad, download **Onavo** from the **App Store**. This compresses your data usage to save you money.

Avoid using apps such as **Facebook**, **Mail**, and especially **Maps**, as these can download huge amounts of data.

Mobile Data Off

USING THE CELL network to receive data while you're in a different country can result in extra charges on your bill.

To turn this off, open *Settings*, *General*, *Cellular*, and slide **Cellular Data** off.

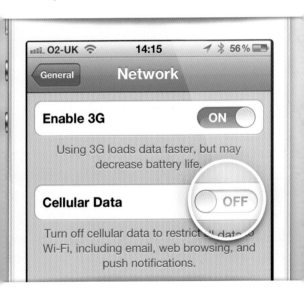

Airplane Mode On

TURNING ON AIRPLANE Mode stops all connections to your cell network or Wi-Fi networks.

This not only saves you money, but you can also use it to stop all calls coming in while you're asleep. If you would still like your notifications to come through, turn on Do Not Disturb, as described in the Advanced chapter, instead.

Change Time Zone

WHEN YOU TRAVEL, your iPhone may automatically change the time based on your current location. However, some carriers don't support this.

To manually change your time zone, open *Settings*, *General*, *Date & Time*. Turn off **Set Automatically** and then select **Time Zone**. Type in your current location and select it from the list. Don't forget to change it back when you get home!

Drop a Pin

WHILE ON HOLIDAY you can use *Maps* to drop a pin and save a small area of the map to memory—for example, the location of your hotel. You'll need to be connected to a Wi-Fi network to do this.

Tap and hold the screen to drop a pin. Zoom in on the pin to get a more detailed map. If you leave the Wi-Fi network to go exploring, the location is still saved so you can find your way back without getting lost.

Bookmark a Location

BOOKMARKING LOCATIONS IN *Maps* means you can find places again easily. It also reduces the time spent connected to the internet in the *Maps* app.

From any pin description, tap the blue arrow and then **Add to Bookmarks**.

Tap the bookmark icon and select from your saved locations to quickly view it on the map again.

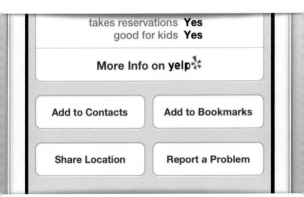

The iPhone 5 sold five million units in its first weekend on sale

CHAPTER SEVENTEEN
ADVANCED

BECOME AN
iPHONE GURU

Do Not Disturb

TURNING ON THE Do Not Disturb setting stops any notification alerts from apps showing on the iPhone. You will still receive notifications, but they are hidden until you unlock your device. To enable this function, open *Settings* and turn on **Do Not Disturb**.

While Do Not Disturb is turned on, a crescent moon is shown in the status bar next to the time.

Schedule Do Not Disturb

YOU CAN SCHEDULE Do Not Disturb to turn on and off automatically at certain times of day.

To do so, open *Settings*, *Notifications*, *Do Not Disturb*, and turn on **Scheduled**. Choose the times you would like Do Not Disturb to be enabled, such as when you're usually asleep or if you have a regular meeting scheduled. Now you won't be disturbed unnecessarily!

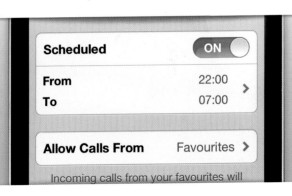

Enabled Phone Calls

WITH DO NOT Disturb turned on, all notifications—including phone calls—will be restricted.

If you would still like phone calls to be enabled, choose from the options under **Allow Calls From**. Choose from **Favorites**, **Everyone**, or **No One** to decide which calls are allowed.

Repeated Calls

YOU CAN ALSO turn on **Repeated Calls**. This means that if the same number calls a second time, it will override the Do Not Disturb and the phone will ring as normal.

This is to make sure that those really important calls get through to you even with Do Not Disturb turned on.

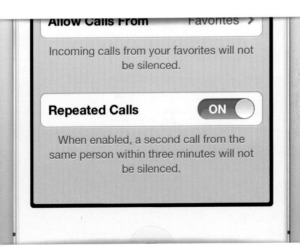

Allow Calls From   Favorites >

Incoming calls from your favorites will not be silenced.

Repeated Calls   ON

When enabled, a second call from the same person within three minutes will not be silenced.

Hide Facebook Contacts

WHEN YOU CONNECT to your Facebook account, your iPhone automatically syncs details with the *Contacts* app. This can make your list of contacts confusing, but there is a way to hide your Facebook contacts.

Tap **Groups** to see a list of your contact groups. Deselect **All Facebook** from the checklist and tap **Done** to return to your contacts list. This should now only show the contacts you've entered on your iPhone.

Dictionary Everywhere

QUICKLY FIND THE definition of any word using the built-in dictionary. While using any apps that allow you to select text, tap and hold a word, then tap the **Define** option.

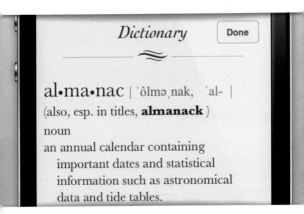

As well as the definition, you also get example uses, phrases that use the word, its origin, and even famous people who have that word as their surname.

Favorites Not Just for Calls

IN THE *PHONE* app, Favorites and **Recents** are great for making quick calls and returning any calls you might have missed. But have you noticed the little blue arrow to the right of each entry in the list?

Tap here for options to call that person back on any of their numbers, send an email or text, or add them to your Favorites list. You can also send contact details via email or MMS.

Mark Errett iPhone	Monday
Mark Errett iPhone	Mon
Hayley mobile	Monday
Sarah mobile	Sunday
Hayley mobile	Saturday

AirPrint

YOU CAN WIRELESSLY print from your iPhone as long as you have an AirPrint enabled printer. If the printer is on the same wireless network, your iPhone will automatically detect it.

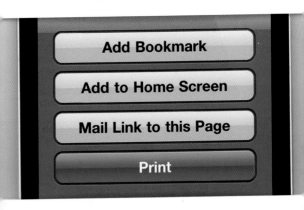

Using this feature, you can print from *Photos*, *Safari*, or *Mail*. Press the arrow icon and then select **Print** to bring up a list of printers. Tap **Print** again to begin printing.

Remind at Location

YOU CAN USE the *Reminders* app to send you an alert when you reach a certain location.

In *Reminders*, tap a reminder and choose from the options. Turn on **Remind Me At a Location** and choose **When I Leave** or **When I Arrive**. Tap the address and choose from the saved addresses or **Enter an Address...** to add a custom location. The phone will alert when you leave or arrive at that location.

Hourly **Weather Forecast**

TAP THE FORECAST in the *Weather* app to switch between a weekly and an hourly forecast.

You can now see if you need a raincoat or sunglasses for the day.

Forward and Delete SMS

YOU CAN FORWARD and delete individual messages, both standard text messages or multimedia messages.

Open a message conversation, tap the **Edit** button, then tap the circles to the left of each message to select them. Then tap **Forward** or **Delete**.

Scientific Calculator

THE USUAL CALCULATOR provides large, easy-to-use buttons for basic arithmetic.

But if you tip the phone sideways, this turns into a scientific calculator, where you can now perform more complex calculations. You can also copy and paste, and if you swipe across the display it deletes the last number you entered.

Contacts Text Tone

YOU CAN SET individual text tones for your contacts so you know who's messaged you without looking.

From **Contacts**, go to the contact entry you want and tap **Edit**. Scroll down until you see **text tone**.

Tap on the **Default** button next to this and then choose a new tone for your contact. Tap **Done** and that person has their own unique text tone.

Birthdays!

ARE YOU ALWAYS forgetting that important birthday? Now you can have the *Calendar* app show birthdays.

First, make sure you've saved your friends' birthdays in their contact information. Then open *Calendar* and tap **Calendars** in the top left. Here is the option for **Birthdays**, which you can tap to turn on or off.

4	5	6	7	8	9	10
11	12	13	14	15	16	17
18	19	20	21	22	23	24
25	26	27	28	1	2	3

🎁 all-day   **Tom's Birthday**

View the Week Ahead

WHEN USING THE *Calendar* app, you can quickly view all your upcoming appointments in a handy week view.

Just hold your iPhone sideways to access the view.

Close the Folder

YOU DON'T HAVE to press the Home button to close a folder.

Just tap any spare screen space either above or below the folder icon.

You can also just tap the folder icon again to close it.

Avoid SMS Embarrassment

USUALLY WHEN A text message arrives the iPhone displays it on the screen, even if your phone is locked.

To keep your messages away from prying eyes, open *Settings*, *Notifications*, *Messages* (before iOS 5, *Settings*, *Messages*). Turn off **Show Preview** to hide the text.

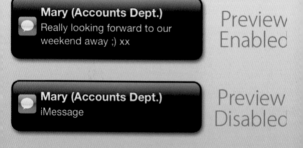

Wi-Fi Hotspot

USING YOUR DATA connection on your iPhone, you can use it as a Wi-Fi hotspot for up to five other devices to use, including iPads and laptops.

To set this up, open **Settings**, *General*, *Cellular*, then *Personal Hotspot*. (If this option isn't available, contact your cell provider.) Once you've switched this on, open **Settings** and you will see the *Personal Hotspot* option near the top.

From here, you'll be asked to set up a password and turn on **Personal Hotspot**. You can then connect your other devices using Wi-Fi, USB cable, or connect Bluetooth.

Home-Click Speed

SOME FEATURES REQUIRE you to press the Home button two or three times in quick succession. However some users may find that they can't press the button quickly enough to get a response. You can change the speed at which your device will register your presses, though.

Open **Settings**, *General*, *Accessibility*, then *Home-click Speed*. From here, choose **Default**, **Slow**, or **Slowest** to change the speed. The iPhone will vibrate to indicate the necessary speed.

See in the **Dark**

THE BUILT-IN LED flash on the iPhone 4 and 4S can be used as a flashlight.

Open the *Camera* app and switch to video mode by sliding the button in the bottom right corner. Then turn on flash from the top left corner.

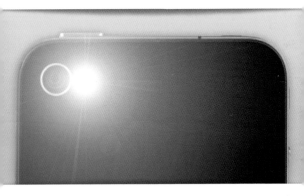

Now you have a personal flashlight— handy for when you're searching for something in the dark!

Apple spent $640 million on advertising for the iPhone in the United States from 2007-2011

CHAPTER EIGHTEEN
TROUBLESHOOTING

SOLVE THE PROBLEM

Pause Downloads

LARGE APPLICATIONS OR updates can sometimes take a long time to download or stall over a data connection, so you might want to pause them while you check your email or browse with *Safari*.

To pause the download, tap the app icon. The progress bar will stop and 'Paused' appears beneath. To continue the download, simply tap the icon again.

Restarting Properly

A HARD-REBOOT CAN be handy if an app refuses to start or if your phone has frozen.

Hold the Home and On/Off buttons together for 10 seconds, ignoring the 'slide to power off' message that appears. The phone will shut down.

Turn it on again normally and it should be working again.

Press and hold the Home and On/Off buttons together

Airplane Mode Shuffle

SOMETIMES IT MIGHT look like there's no signal available on your phone when you're pretty sure there should be.

Simply turning your phone off and on again can bring it back to life and get a signal, but there's an even quicker way.

From *Settings* turn *Airplane Mode* on and then off again This restarts the network circuitry and often finds that missing signal.

Hold to Quit the App

WHEN AN APP becomes unresponsive, you can reset it. Close the app, then from the multitasking bar, tap and hold any icon until the ⊖ symbol appears. Tap this to close the app. Open the app again and it should now be working.

Restoring Apps

YOU CAN DELETE apps from your device and then install them again for no extra charge, if you find they are not working properly.

Open the *App Store*, tap the **Updates** icon and then **Purchased**. Tap **Not On This iPhone** to see a list of apps that you have deleted from your device. Tap **Install** or the cloud icon to download that app again.

The Apple iPhone Keyboard supports 44 languages

CHAPTER NINETEEN
HAVE YOU NOTICED?

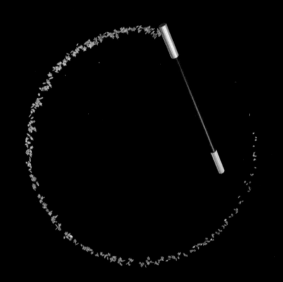

NEAT LITTLE TOUCHES

Updating **Calendar Icon**

FAR FROM BEING a static image to launch the calendar, the icon actually updates to show the current day and date.

Glancing at the home screen is a great way of finding out the date without having to look at a calendar.

Automatic Pause

IF YOU ARE listening to music with headphones, and you pull them out of the iPhone, playback is automatically paused.

To start the music again, plug the headphones back in and press the middle button on the headset.

Is That You **Bono?**

WHEN USING THE *Music* app you may have noticed the Artists icon and thought nothing of it.

Look closer, though, and you'll see that it's a silhouette of Bono, the lead singer of the group U2.

Automatic Recognition

IN CERTAIN APPLICATIONS, including *Mail* and *Notes*, your phone will underline anything that looks like an address or telephone number.

Tapping a phone number dials it and by tapping an address you can view that location directly in the *Maps* application.

Maps Icon

IF YOU LOOK closely you'll see that the *Maps* app icon is actually where the Apple headquarters are in Cupertino, California.

Known as Infinite Loop for being a continuous oval, this has been the location of Apple's campus since 1993. An infinite loop is also a common type of programming error, so is apt as a name for the road.

Flyover

IF YOU ARE using the satellite view in the *Maps* app, you can see high detailed 3D images of certain cities around the world.

If you can access Flyover, the 3D button changes to a skyscraper icon. Tap this and the camera angle changes. You can then pan around and zoom in to see famous landmarks and buildings.

Tilt to **Shine**

WHILE IN NOW Playing view in the *Music* app, you'll see a volume slider along the bottom with a silver button. If you tilt your iPhone left or right, the reflection on the button changes depending on the angle of your tilt.

Spotlight the Folder

AFTER YOU'VE PLACED an app in a folder, you might forget where you've placed it. You can find the app using Spotlight, which will locate it and tell you which folder it's in.

You can open the app direct from Spotlight, but you'll know where the app is when you want to open it in future.

Tips & Tricks
**iPhone
Secrets**

Available on the
App Store

Tips & Tricks
**iPad
Secrets**

Available on the
App Store

Thank You!

KEEP IN TOUCH and share your iPhone experiences with us. We also would like to hear from you how you think we can improve our guides!

Get in touch with us at the following places:

 facebook.com/tipstricksguides

 @iphonetipsters

 info@intelligenti.com

WRITER MARK ERRETT	**LEAD DESIGNER** TOM OXLADE
DEVELOPMENT MANAGER MARK WHITE	**DESIGNER** CHRIS TYLER

DIRECTOR
JON BONNICK

intelligenti